CLIVE GIBSON

authorHOUSE

AuthorHouse™ UK
1663 Liberty Drive
Bloomington, IN 47403 USA
www.authorhouse.co.uk
Phone: UK TFN: 0800 0148641 (Toll Free inside the UK)
UK Local: (02) 0369 56322 (+44 20 3695 6322 from outside the UK)

© 2025 Clive Gibson. All rights reserved.

No part of this book may be reproduced, stored in a retrieval system, or transmitted by any means without the written permission of the author.

Published by AuthorHouse 05/09/2025

ISBN: 979-8-8230-8897-8 (sc)
ISBN: 979-8-8230-8898-5 (e)

Print information available on the last page.

Any people depicted in stock imagery provided by Getty Images are models, and such images are being used for illustrative purposes only. Certain stock imagery © Getty Images.

This book is printed on acid-free paper.

Because of the dynamic nature of the Internet, any web addresses or links contained in this book may have changed since publication and may no longer be valid. The views expressed in this work are solely those of the author and do not necessarily reflect the views of the publisher, and the publisher hereby disclaims any responsibility for them.

CONTENTS

Preface vii
Dedication ix

Chapter 1 What If? 1
Chapter 2 Hard Times 15
Chapter 3 Relocation 23
Chapter 4 Becoming A Man 56
Chapter 5 The Business 73
Chapter 6 The Start of the F.I.T. Club 78
Chapter 7 The End Game 101

PREFACE

What follows is an autobiography, focusing on my own life experiences, reactions, and observations, which have provided me a feeling of worth.

If what I have written seems to come across as somewhat self-absorbed, this is the reason why.

I have put into words my actions, my feelings, my contributions that together made for what I believe to be a great life.

I would like to think that my readers will be inspired to just be nice and helpful to others, to work hard, and never give up.

DEDICATION

This book is dedicated to everyone who has been part of my life, without whom I could not have had so happy and fulfilling a journey.

I would particularly like to thank Angela my wife who has played a pivotal part of the last 25 years, my daughter Tyrina, and my son Kevin, who also have spent unlimited amounts of time and effort to not only achieve what they have but to help me achieve my dreams and become successful, not only in business but in life itself.

CHAPTER 1

WHAT IF?

I was born on the 17th of January 1959, a twin to a sister, Tyrina, and part of a family of me, two brothers, and including Tyrina five sisters. But when just three months old, my twin and I were diagnosed with pneumonia – sadly, Tyrina lost her battle and died. I was told that I must have been the stronger twin, and from time to time, I wonder how she would have turned out!

I was born in Fawdon, Newcastle, and we left the area when I was six or seven years old. I can't remember this place, but I do remember being told that we were all taken to the Civic Centre council office with my Mam and all my sisters, my Mam saying to whoever it was behind the counter, 'You can tell them that I will not be leaving until you give me and my family somewhere better to live.' Not that I would have known, but at that time we had been evicted because my Dad put all the windows out of the next door neighbours' house, calling them 'toffee-nose cowards' as he wanted to fight the man of the house, but he would not come out. This all erupted because they had seen my eldest brother Bobby, who'd run away from borstal (young offenders institute), sneaking into our house, and the neighbour then called the police. Bobby was well known in the area for his villainy, which would include fighting, shoplifting, burglary. He would never back down in a fight, but always done his best to take care of us kids and look after Mam.

Mam just got us huddled all together and said, 'Whatever happens, you do not let go of each other.' The council offered Mam a place in Walker, a shithole – well, the fun began, with the council staff in the end calling the police and the welfare people to get us off the premises. Mam stuck to her guns and said, 'Want us to leave? Then have a heart, you know you have better places for us.'

What if?

Mam battled on, talking to the welfare and the police for ages, then the welfare people done a deal with the council, and asked for us to be moved to Benwell. It was quite a rough place, many disadvantaged families were put there, and this is where my childhood proper began, in a three-bedroom, upper-floor flat, a 'Tyneside Flat' as known, with a yard and outside toilet. Our bath night was done in a big tin tub, and being the youngest, I was left with the dirty water. The scullery was tiny, small gas stove with an oven. Our back door led down a flight of stairs to the yard and the loo, then the yard gate went directly to the back lane where a lot of our playtime was spent.

My Dad was a military man to the bone. He fought in the Second World War and in Korea. He was a hard man, liked a drink, loved his garden, liked his betting on the horses, never winning much if I remember right. He always turned out for the Remembrance Day or 'Poppy Day' parade. As a family, we were always by the roadside to watch and support our Dad march past with such pride in the battalion of the Fusiliers he was in. After the parade, we would all go back to the barracks where there was free food and pop while our Dad had a pint or two of lager. I remember him being very upset when he was told to hand in his uniform, or demobbed as it was. He was always telling me, 'Son, when you are old enough, join the army and become a PTI [physical training instructor],' as I was a very fit boy and enjoyed all sports.

My mother was a very quiet woman – 'til she had to pull it out – and very hard-working, always trying her best to scrape through day by day. She worked in the coalmine pit canteen as a cook and liked a game of bingo, just trying to win some money for the family to eat. When she would win, she had a gonk, a troll doll that the head would pull off and she'd hide some of her winnings in the body, away from Dad.

At the weekend, my Dad used to go for a pint along the Scotswood Road to the Crooked Billet pub, well known for being very rough, fights breaking out all the time. My Mam would give my oldest sister, Denise (14 years old at the time), about two shillings, or 25 pence now, to take Maureen (12), Angela (11), Pamela (9), and me (7) to the flicks, to see a movie. We would all pile

What if?

in, Denise being in charge – she'd would make sure me and Pamela were away from each other as we would just mess about. Though we only lived about five minutes walk away, after the show, we would wait inside until our Mam collected us. We would get in, and if Mam had won at bingo, we would have a couple of bags of chips between us, then bed. If not, then bed and wait for Dad to come in, who would always have crisps and nuts to share. Pamela, always being his favourite, would get the first pick, and the most, and then we were all back to bed.

My Dad was a hard-working man. During our time in Benwell, he was a night watchman on the roads, making sure that all the paraffin lamps were lit, and no one was nicking any tools. Mam from time to time made toffee apples and toffee cakes, some with hundreds and thousands on top, the families with kids came from all over the area to buy them, ha'penny for a toffee cake and a penny for a toffee apple. With them she used to have a jumble sale with all the spare clothes from her coats and dresses, Dad's jackets, Denise's clothes, anything that was possible to sell, so a few bobs was made doing this.

Clive Gibson

Being the youngest always allowed me to get away with a lot of things. Pamela and I would play truant from school and would often run up the high-rise flats and steal milk tokens from under the used bottles, then run back down the 15 flights. The pop man came on a Tuesday, we would hide until the driver went into the flats with his deliveries, grab a crate of pop (which was heavy for us), and hide around the garages until he got back into his van and drove off. We carried a few bottles of pop home and then go back for the rest; it made an easier explanation if we were carrying only one or two bottles if we bumped into a policeman! When we got home, my mother would often go berserk as she thought we were at school, but she calmed down when we give her the milk tokens and bottles of pop. Times were very hard for a family of seven kids!

As well as my other three sisters, Denise, Maureen, and Angela, were my two brothers: Bobby, the oldest, and David, who spent time in a care home as he was caught being an accessory to stealing a handbag. Bobby loved having a younger brother like me. Since I was about five years old he'd have me practise boxing, putting his hands up and getting me to punch them, always saying, 'If anyone picks on you and your sisters, this is what you do.' When he came home, he would also look out for my Mam. However, unbeknownst to me, when Bobby was home, it was usually because he was on the run. Police would often call at the house looking for him. When this happened, there was a drill that we would all follow – all the kids (five of us) jumped into bed, and Bobby would curl up into a ball in the middle of the bed, this way the police could not see him. My mother would do her nut with the police for disturbing us, and so they would just leave.

Even at seven years old I was very aware of the struggle my family endured, so we all tried to do our best to help out, bring some type of income into the family home. Pamela and I were into anything and everything to try and make a penny or two. Around this time, most of the houses in Scotswood, part of the Benwell catchment, were being demolished amid the whole post-war redevelopments going on all over the place, so there were plenty of things to be got and sold. We used to go into the empty houses and rip out the lead piping, rediffusion cables for the copper wire, even take the lead clasps that held the wire up. I distinctly remember one time when me, Pamela, and our friend David Luckheart were in the houses, we each took turns to hang out the windows while the others held on to our feet. There were no floors or ceilings, only the wooden rafters were left, along which we used to move from one end to the other.

We decided to climb up to the loft area to break the metal gutter down, but while we were moving the roof tiles a bloke from three doors down saw us and started shouting, *I know what you little bastards are up to and I'm going to call the police, so get out now!*, so Pamela, David, and I ran across the rafters to hide, us two boys jumping into two empty slots next to the chimney breast – but Pamela lost her footing and fell through the gap in the rafters. She was three floors up with lots of broken glass and bricks down below, and it was by pure luck that she was caught by the sleeve of her coat. That was one of the scariest moments of my life, seeing her hanging there by a nail. I jumped out of my hole – the bloke three doors down was still shouting and swearing at us – but Pamela was too heavy for me to pull on my own, she was screaming and crying, and I was in a blind panic. I shouted at David to come and give me a hand, but he was scared rigid in his hiding hole, shouting at me to leave her in case we all got caught. I lost my temper and screamed at him if he did not come and help, I would kick his fucking head off. That done the trick, and he came out and helped pull Pamela to safety. We waited for the man to stop shouting, then we got down and collected the bits and pieces we had got earlier to sell. This all went on during the time we lived in Brunell Terrace in Benwell.

One time, we even pinched a slab of lead from the church roof. This was quite a task due to the sheer size and weight, it took us nearly three days to get this down, but eventually, after a lot of hard work, it rolled off the roof and fell to the ground. We had to then roll it down the street without being seen or caught. Eventually, we got it home, my Mam once again done her nut with us, mainly because she feared we would get hurt or caught, then sent away like our Bobby. Our Dad cut the lead into strips ready for Fatty the rag-and-bone man to come. The rag man came once a week to see what we had to sell. He bought the lead for five shillings, my Dad gave my Mam two shillings and sixpence, and Pamela and I got three pennies each – we were over the Moon! We went straight up to the sweet shop and bought bags and bags of sweets. That was the start of our little business venture.

We started wagging off school; being truant was made easier as when we went back to school, Mam would give us a letter saying we'd been ill. There was good money in scrap and at the derelict houses; once the coast was clear we pulled drainpipes off, also the windows were on pulleys with weights on the end of a string, so we took them weights as well. At the end of the day, we had about a ton of scrap for Fatty and lots of money for my Mam.

We then spotted a lot of black smoke and saw the council workers burning some kind of rubber or plastic, and then they would pull loads of wire from the flames. As I watched this process, I then told Pamela to ask Dad what it was and if it was worth anything. He told us it was copper wire from the TV cables. Later, we watched with great curiosity to see where the council workers were getting it from and, after they burned it, where they were hiding the copper. Well, it wasn't long before we saw the workers pulling the black wire from the walls under the windows outside, going from one black box to another, and then they were storing it in an empty house further down the road. While we were from night to night getting copper from the water pipes and brass fittings from the gas pipes for our little store of scrap, we would also go and nick some of the council's wire, as we knew they could not say anything, as they were stealing it themselves. This kind of thing went on for most, if not all my time in Benwell.

On the odd occasion when I went to school, I was quite good at standing on my head, doing handsprings, and walking on my hands, so I used to practise in the break times, always drawing an audience. A lot of the kids would ask me to do a headstand as they thought it was great. Some of them used to try but keep falling over, I was forever giving advice on the best way to do it – perhaps this was the start of my career in becoming a PTI.

Around 1963 or '64, there was a building just being put up along from where we lived. It was the

Cruddas Park shopping centre, which must have taken two years or more to finish, and Pamela and I used to investigate the site to see if there were any goodies to be had to sell or use. Pamela had two good friends, Susan (or Sooty as we called her), and Valerie, same age as Pamela, so both 18 months or so older than me. When I was about eight years old, it was with Sooty I had my first sexual experience, on the Cruddas Park building site. Pamela, Sooty, Sooty's brother Steven, and I were messing about having a great time throwing sand, cement, and whatever was lying about, then as it got a little darker around 5 pm Pamela was with Steven and I was left with Sooty, who asked if I would like to kiss her. I was a very shy boy, so it took me by surprise as she was older and very pretty. She kept saying, 'Pamela is doing it over there, come on, lie down here and I will just kiss you.' I was on my back under this plastic covering, used to keep the sand and cement dry. Sooty then started kissing my lips and rubbing my private parts on top of my shorts, asking me to play with her. She put my hand down her knickers, and asked me to move my fingers, I was so nervous and felt her getting all wet. Sooty was saying, 'Do you want to put your cock in?' as she was rubbing faster and harder, she then pulled me on top of her, and ask me to push with my hips, as she was pulling me towards her and pushing herself against me, not sure what I was doing as she was doing all the movements. I pushed myself off and stood up quickly, got my shorts up. Pamela came across to ask if I was OK, then said we better get home as it was getting really dark. We all walked back to our streets and said we would see each other the following night.

This experience did not happen again with Sooty as her family was one of the first to be moved out as the council began to empty the streets to demolish more houses and flats. As we lived in the upper flat we had a downstair neighbour for a couple of years, then they moved out, and as the council was going to demolish the place they did not have a tenant to put in, so it stayed empty. Pamela and I took advantage of the storage. One time, Pamela, Valerie, David Luckheart, and I were hanging about in the downstair flat and we decided to have a striptease. Pamela was first, she got down to her vest and knickers, and then Valerie was next, who went the whole way – completely naked – this was brilliant as now I could see what I had been touching with Sooty! But before anything happened, my Mam called us in for dinner. And that was my second experience with girls.

Otherwise, Bobby was always saying to me, 'Anyone calls you chicken, beat them up.' He was so proud of me, always showing me off to his pals, getting me to do a handstand or a handspring. This was great for me as his pals were always giving me a couple of pennies for sweets. He used to take me to town with him, and we would meet up with his pals in cafés, and while he was doing business I would be given an ice cream and a glass of pop. On the odd occasion we would be walking around Woolworths, and Bobby and his pals would be giving me sweets, chocolate bars to eat. Little did I know they had not paid for them! They used to laugh a lot, really having a good time.

CHAPTER 2

HARD TIMES

There was a time Pamela and I were playing in the front street, and looking amongst all the rubble from the houses that had been knocked down for bits and pieces, wire, lead pipes, things like that, when my mate David Luckheart turned up and asked if he could also play with us. Pamela said no, so he then started shouting and calling Pamela names. Bobby's bedroom window opened and he shouted down to me, ' You're not going to let him talk to your sister like that – chin him there on the bricks!' So I shouted to David, 'Come over here and I will kick your face in.' He said he'd fight me on the grass down there. I looked up at Bobby, still at the window, and he shouted, *Get him there on the bricks*, David shouted, *On the grass – unless you're frightened,* then Bobby shouted, *Go on, go down on the grass – if you lose, you will get a good hiding off me.*

Off we went down the road a little way from our house to a level grass part outside the school. We started fighting, grabbing onto each other, trying to get each other to the ground somehow. David got my finger in his mouth and started to bite – that was painful, Pamela shouting, *Come on Clive, knock his head off, smash his face in*! Somehow I managed to pull his head towards me and headbutt him, which made him let go of my finger. Then I lost my temper. I knocked him down as he was still crying from the headbutt, and kicked and punched him 'til he said, 'OK, OK, I've had enough.'

As Pamela and I were walking back up the street, I was really trying my hardest not to show I was crying with the pain of my finger. But as this wasn't the last fight I'd have, and what I found over the years when people did pick a fight with me and then got hurt and start crying and saying they're sorry, they've had enough, that only made me more angry. What did they think would happen? They start it, they assume I'm weak or can be beat, they're wrong, I show 'em, but I lose my temper, too. Not just as I need to get rid of my frustration, but it's disappointment in their performance. I'm hurt, but I'm willing to fight on, and there's them all sorry now.

Anyway, we get back to the flat, Pamela shouting up to Bobby, *He's crying*, I was saying, *No I'm not, big mouth*. Bobby then said, 'Well done, don't ever let people talk to any of your sisters like that,' and then he said 'Catch!' and tossed a half-crown down to me. 'That's for a good job, well done.' That made the pain go away, and me and Pamela went straight up the shop for sweets and crisps, as we used to share all our money, but I think this was the first time I did not spend it all. I give Pamela a shilling, and I spent a shilling and kept sixpence to save, as money was so hard to come by, this seemed a good idea, as this meant I would always have something.

When I was nine, I remember this day at school, and still to this day I feel angry about it. I did not really spend a lot of time at school, but did more when Bobby was home – he'd walk me to school to make sure I got an education, stayed out of trouble, got a good job. There were about

15 other kids in the class, most I did not really know, and the teacher was asking kids to stand up and tell the class what they had for breakfast, and they were all saying things like, *I had a bowl of cornflakes*, or *bacon sandwich*, and so on and on. All I'd had was a slice of toast, but to fit in with what everyone else was saying I tried to lie and say that I had sausage and egg. But when I tried to say sausage, it came out like, 'Slosage'. The teacher asked me to say it again, and I did – 'Slosage.' And the teacher asked me to say it again, kept going at me, and the harder I tried, the worse it got, and the whole class was laughing, even the teacher was really enjoying seeing me embarrassed. The more I was laughed at, the more bad I felt, like my mouth was so dry, my face was on fire with embarrassment, I was shaking, and felt I needed to do something as it was not going to stop.

'Fuck off!', I yelled at the teacher, ran out of school, up the street home, crying. My Mam was in and asked what was wrong, and I just told her I would not be going back to that place. She grabbed me by the arms and asked, 'What is wrong, why are you crying?' So I told her. She put her coat on and dragged me screaming back down to the school, and then got me to show her the classroom and point out the teacher. I felt still upset and a little frightened, but thought that this was going to be good, because this was my Mam. And there she was, saying to the teacher that he was not allowed to make kids feel like this, as his job is to teach and encourage, not to mock – and then give him a slap across the face.

This also happened to Maureen, my middle sister, at her senior school a week later. The teacher was making fun of her being a little overweight, and my Mam went in to sort this out. This time, it was in the schoolyard at break time, all the kids were out, walking about, chatting in small groups. It was a woman teacher, full of herself, trying to put the situation that she said it to encourage Maureen to be aware of what she was eating, to help with her weight. Not according to my Mam. The teacher got the same treatment that my teacher got, a good old slap across the face. The kids went crazy with laughter, teacher ran off into the school, very upset. As my Mam walked off she was saying, 'Never take the piss out of my family.'

There were times we would go into town, Denise in charge of us all, Maureen, Angela, Pamela, me and David Luckheart, Susan (Sooty), and Valerie, we would get on the bus at the top of the street. It was about 10 stops into town, and when the bus conductor would come up the stairs to the upper deck, we would all be sitting at the back of the bus. Two or three stops would have passed, and by the time he got to us and ask for the fare, Denise would start with, '*She's* got it,' pointing to Maureen, then she says, 'No, *he's* got it,' pointing to David, and so on, until it ended up back at Denise, by this time we were almost at the town, and only then the conductor realised he was not getting paid and would kick us off the bus but we were already at the town. And then we would do the same going back home. It was a great laugh.

Other times is when we had our bogeys out, go-karts made of two big pram wheels, and one small scooter wheel at the front, all tied together with string. Starting at the top of Clumber Street, leading straight downhill to Scotswood Road, we must have been doing about 30 miles an hour down this hill. To get up, we used to hang on the back of any wagon that was going up the hill, mostly council trucks. The drivers were quite good at times, slowing down so we could get a hold properly for a tow. Then there were the other drivers trying to speed up past us, but we always had a backup. One of the lasses started to walk across the road at the same time we were trying to get a hold of the wagon, the drivers used to do their nut, shouting and screaming, stopping the wagon and jumping out, trying to scare us – well it just made things so funny seeing him run around the wagon trying to catch one or two of us, anyway as he got back in his truck and we would all climb back on.

Then there were times just hanging around the back lane playing hide and seek, kick the can, and as it got a little later and darker, we would all head off home for our dinner and a couple of times a week, a wash. My Mam and Dad had to put this tin bath by the fire and fill it with the kettle and pans heated from the gas cooker. As there were five of us, I was always last to get in. Then supper and bed. We were all good, close friends, and had some great times. Weekends were always fun, going into the old houses and finding loads of things that people who had moved out had left. Pamela and I found a gramophone and hundreds of 78 RPM records, we stood for hours just snapping the records into two or three pieces or putting them in a big pile ready for throwing them like a Frisbee, seeing who could get the furthest. Meanwhile, the council were demolishing the area, and one by one, families were moving out to different areas. We were the last ones in the street to leave, there was just our house left standing and the church in the whole street.

It got pretty boring now all our friends had left, I still went wandering around looking for things that were good to sell. I found this pipe, very heavy, so I struggled with it for about a half a mile, but just as I got to the back lane going up to my back door, a policeman shouted, *What have you got there?* I dropped it and ran into the house. He knocked on the door, Mam opened the door to find this policeman there asking to see the little lad who had just run in. My Mam done her best to say I was not there, but he'd seen me run in, and said he's stolen lead pipes and is under arrest for stealing lead pipes. I could have been, as I had just turned 10 years old, but my Mam told him I was too young, as I was only eight, so too young to arrest. Instead, he give me a good telling off and off he went, shaking his head.

CHAPTER 3

RELOCATION

We were the last people in our street in Benwell for four, five month, before we were then relocated to Blakelaw, about five miles away, we lived in a four-bedroom house in a cul-de-sac. It was a lovely area and we found all our old friends living in the same part, but most or all the families living here were considered 'problem families' – and it was going to be hard to go to school as this was filled with a lot of undesirables brought in from local areas: Montague, Kenton, Kenton Bar, Cowgate, and Blakelaw – the council had this idea of putting problem families into good areas in the hope it'd rub off on them, but 'good' families moved out while problem families moved in, recreating the problem all over again.

Clive Gibson

At Montague school, I thought I needed to dig in and stick with it, and no playing truant. I was good at sports, so that was where I put most of my energy, but I was not good at football, even though my two brothers were at county level. My best assets were my hands; I had good eye-to-hand coordination. I made the rounders team, and I became the best at batting and the best catcher. I was really very proud and chuffed with myself as up until this point I was all alone, so when I was given my strip to play for the school, my God, I was the best team member you could have asked for. I turned up at all the home and away games, and we did very well in the schools' league.

One day, though, I was due to play an away game of rounders and I was really looking forward to it. But during the day I was doing work on the school gardening project, they got me turning over rocks and stones with this garden fork. It slipped, and stabbed me in my foot. Because we were so poor, I wasn't in decent boots, just had plastic sandals on. There was blood everywhere, so I was sent to the school nurse. My PE teacher came to see me and said I could not play in the evening match

What if?

as I had to go home and rest. It absolutely broke my heart, I remember breaking down and crying, saying that I was OK, I could play, but my teacher said *rules are rules,* and I needed to go home. I felt totally let down by this, I was just a lad trying to do his best and what he was good at, and did not play another game from then on. It was after that incident that I thought of competing in other sporting activities, hockey and athletics were my choice of sport at my junior school.

I decided to try and get a Saturday job for a little pocket money, and began walking around with my bucket and a sponge, knocking on doors asking if they wanted their car washed. I got a couple done at 25 pence a car, then I asked this lady who was just pulling up in her drive, and jackpot! She said, 'Yes, and if you do a good job, I would like it done every week.' She was a music teacher at Ponteland High School. Mrs. Young was her name. I really made a good job of it, and the following week was again a good job. She asked me if I would like a drink, and took me into her kitchen, asking a little about me, my school, where I lived, what my Mam and Dad done for a living, brothers and sisters, she got the whole picture of my background. She then gave me a cup of coffee with brown sugar and goat's milk – it was the best hot drink I had ever had. Then, after washing the car every week, we had coffee and biscuits.

Mrs Young also asked me to wash her windows and frames, and she increased my pay to £1, 50 pence for the car and 50 pence for the windows. She also made rugs, and started to show me how to do it from a piece of vinyl, sewing the wool through and making a pattern, it was brilliant, then she started playing music on her piano while we had coffee and biscuits.

Mrs. Young was a widow, having lost her husband in a car accident, as this is why I think she liked my company for a couple of hours. She said I would do very well in life as I was a hard worker and a very nice person. We parted company a few years later as I joined the army, but always we were keeping in touch until her passing 22 years later. God Bless.

Running around the streets in Blakelaw was great fun, there was always something to do, play football, kick the can, knockie-nine doors, or catchy-kissy as I'd play with this girl Dawn. She was one of Pamela's friends whose family had moved in across the street a few months earlier than us, and who Pamela was always trying to pair me up with – it worked, and we dated on and off over the years into my teens.

We also went out of the area and find some orchards where my friends and I would nick the fruits. I also had a fair few fights. I had quite a good reputation for sticking up for myself at junior school and around the streets, and having a go at anyone who tried their luck with me. I was in the Kenton Mad Mob and Montague Warriors as most of the people I hung around with were from Kenton, and there were a lot of gang fights, gangs from all areas coming to the fields or on the Town Moor to have mass scraps, get stuck in, but if the police were ever spotted someone always said so and we'd all scarper all directions – no one dobbed anyone to the law.

At 11, I went to senior school at Slatyford High, where my brother David and sister Angela went. David had left well before I arrived, and Angela was in the fifth form; it was Angela that kept me going to school for a full year with only one half-day off. My end-of-year report was Bs and Cs, which was fantastic for me as I was really eager to learn.

My other sister Pamela went to Blakelaw High School but got expelled and transferred to Slatyford High – that's when everything went wrong for my learning, as Pamela was such an undisciplined young girl, always looking for trouble, we often played truant and went home. Such that I was brought up before the truancy board, and they informed me they would not accept me missing school – or not too much of it, as they said, I was a very polite young man and had the ability to do very well. I thought about this, and afterwards I went to all the lessons that had a register and done a bunk for the others. Games was always in the afternoon with a registration so had to go to all of these but I enjoyed every lesson because it was sport where I excelled, becoming captain for the cross-country, swimming, hockey, softball, and rugby teams – never missed a game – and enjoyed my trampolining, eventually coming sixth in the North East championships in 1971 – as well as gymnastics, athletics, and even though I only played a couple of games in defence at football in the B team it was still good fitness.

It was when I was 12 in high school in the second year that I had my first serious fight, and things changed after that. It was over tattoos – as I did not have any. A pal of mine called Robert Morgan had Indian ink dots on his knuckles and a couple of crap tattoos on his arms. As I was walking back to my desk in technical drawing class, he said that I was too chicken to have any tattoos. Now, Bobby always said, 'If anyone ever calls you a chicken, then you must beat them up.' So I asked him why he was sitting with his sleeves rolled up, showing his shit tattoos off, 'cos when I was old enough I would get proper tattoos. As expected, he jumped up to have a go at me and he tried to kick me in my privates – but his foot got caught in my trousers and I punched him in the face three times. The teacher then came over and broke the fight up and sent us to the headmaster's office. I thought that we both would get punished with the belt or ruler across our hands, but Mr. Hackett our headmaster was angry with me, as he considered me to be a good person with a good future, same he said for my sister Angela and brother David, and I'd never been in trouble before. He said if he ever saw me again at his office, I would be severely punished. But he didn't give me a chance to put my side of the story, that it wasn't my fault, and I was merely retaliating and defending myself. We were both sent back to class, and I thought that was that.

After the afternoon break, I decided to go home, or at least to my brother Bobby's, who was living a few miles away with his girlfriend, Sally. The school bell rang for lunchtime when I was talking to my pal Harry, telling him I was going home and to cover for me by telling the teacher at registration I was feeling unwell. I walked up to the bus stop, bus came, I got on up to the top deck, sitting in the middle. I hadn't noticed anyone on the bus … but then I heard laughter and whispering, and I heard someone say, *Oh yes, he's the teacher's pet, he's such a soft shit*. I turned around and saw Robert Morgan, lain back against the back window, chewing gum and making his mouth go. Then he started shouting, 'Do you want another go?'

I replied, 'I didn't have the first go,' but if he wanted to get off at my stop, then I would finish it.

We got to my stop. I said, 'This is my stop. Are you ready?'

'Why your stop and not mine?' he says. He showed he was ready to bottle it, but his pals then started saying, *Get off at our stop* (which was about three, four mile away) so I said it was no good me going further as I had only paid to this stop, even thinking while waiting for the bus to stop, 'Give him a chance as he's not as good as you.' As the bus stopped, I got off and walked sideways down to the bus stop, one of those metal ones, and I was just about to turn around and say we'd go over to the field when I felt a punch to the side of my head. I was a little dazed but remember saying, 'You fucking cheat,' then grabbed him, pulled him to the ground, landed on top of him and then started to work with my right hand punching him in the head and face whilst holding him down with my knee. He was screaming like a little girl and trying to kick me in the back of the head. After a minute or so, he gave up, I dragged him up off the ground and punched him a couple of more times.

He started crying, saying he was sorry and would never do anything again to me. I was holding the back of his head and he was leaning forward with his hands to his face, but because he was being such a hard man at the school and on the back of the bus – and he cheated while I was getting off the bus – I decided to make him pay a little more to make sure he would never come at me again. I told him: 'Take your hands away from your face and stand up straight,' and as hard as I could (bearing in mind I was only 12) I smashed his face against the bus stop three times. As he fell to the ground I asked if he was sorry now, he was blubbering on saying he was sorry. There was blood everywhere. I did get a little fright seeing the state of him, and offered him his bus fare home, but he said he would just walk to his sister's around the corner. So we shook hands and went our separate ways.

When I got to Bobby and Sally's house, she asked what happened and why was my hand covered in blood. I told her, and she said, 'Go and get a shower and go to bed!' She told me later that night that she could tell I was in shock. Sally later told my brother Bobby, who at this time was a coalman driving four-ton wagons, what had happened, and he was really pleased – I'd stood up for myself and hadn't backed down.

The next morning, I was late getting up, even missed my bus to school, so I said I'd go in in the afternoon. But about 10:30 am, there was a very loud knock on the door. 'I know that knock,' Sally said, 'That's the police.' When she opened the door, it was CID who had come to arrest me for actual bodily harm, or ABH, on Robert. The soft shit had gone to his sister's and told her that I had beat him up for his money, the police went to the school to find my address and then to my Mam's house where they found out I was staying with Bobby and Sally (which was why it took them until mid-morning to find me). Fortunately, Bobby was off that day, and he told me to admit nothing, tell them exactly what had happened – but miss out the bit about smashing his head on the bus stop.

Anyways, it went to the magistrate's court. My Mam and Dad, who did not have a lot of money, borrowed some from a friend and bought me a suit, a purple flare suit, which I wore to court.

I must have looked quite smart, even though I did not feel like it. But Robert Morgan sat to the right of me on a chair in the middle of the court, and when I looked at him, he was dressed like a tramp: jeans, T-shirt, and a little bomber jacket, all of which I somehow knew went in my favour. His solicitor was asking me questions, and me being myself, I answered, *Yes sir, no sir*, saying *sir* after every sentence.

He did not like this at all. 'Just answer yes or no – do not try to win this court over by being polite with sir after every word.'

I said, 'Sorry sir,' (!) and I could tell he was trying to put me down as a thug. But the court found me not guilty, and Robert had to pay the court costs.

The next day at school, I was treated like a hero. Robert was transferred to another school. But then, as much as I tried to get back to learning, I couldn't concentrate. I was only interested in sports and threw myself more into that.

The other side of being a hero was people seeing you different in other ways. Most of the kids in the lower years were afraid of you, same year kids respected you, and older years look at you as someone who will have a go and not give in. I was full glow. I was always ready to stick up for myself, but you have to stay hard, willing, be game for anything, and from now on, it got tougher. Only the older hard lads respected my size and ability – as reputation goes, I was (in their opinion) someone you don't mess with.

For all that though, I was still, I felt, very quiet, shy. When aged 12, 13, I wasn't bothering involving myself with most other people, but had a couple of pals, Harry Wall and Sid Mulholland, as the lads I walked around with. Harry was always very smart, he had top-of-the-range skinhead gear, a Harrington jacket under his blazer, a checked Brutus shirt, two-tone trousers, and red rider boots. Sid was more like me – he could not afford any of these fashion items so just school kit and blazers that in the day had a yellow lining to identify your Mam and Dad as on benefits, and you got free school meals, but because we were now considered the hard boys of the second year no one said anything.

I had a few more fights at school, two are worth talking about. In my third year, this girl called

Clive Gibson

Gail Donaldson, originally from Canada, fancied me, but this lad in a different house fancied her. So he thought he would have a go and get cocky with me, I guess maybe because I was only 4' 11" tall and he was near 6'. During games, he said to me, 'If you even look at her, I will smash your face in.' Well, that sounded like a challenge, so I asked her if I could walk her home from school. She was over the Moon and obviously said yes.

The next day, he caught me between classes and said he was going to get me at dinner time by the music hall. Fine, I said.

I turned up on time, but he didn't, so I thought that was the end of that, then close to 3:30 pm when I was going into my last lesson we passed again in the corridor, he told me he had been sent to the headmaster's during lunch, so I said after school then? He agreed.

It was winter and there was ice and snow on the ground. I was dressed like my granddad; my topcoat was a Crombie, I had my blazer, cardigan, shirt, and tie. He turned up with a couple of friends whereas my pals had to leave to go and catch their bus, but before they did, they told me, *He's a wanker so make it quick, we'll see you in the morning* – and off they went. So here we were. This lad was quite big and athletic with his mates, and me, short, with a skinhead, but very athletic. 'So you fancy your chances then?' I said. He told me I was a tramp and would never be good enough for Gail. I told him, 'Give me a minute while I get ready,' and proceeded to take off my Crombie, my blazer, my tie, and cardigan, folded them in a neat little pile against the wall. This frustrated the hell out of him. Then I said, 'Come on, then,' and he grabbed and pushed me to the ground.

Because it was icy, I couldn't keep my balance, and he landed on top of me, his face was above mine – I headbutted him on the nose and pushed him off me. I then got on my feet and started kicking him in the ribs. His pals started to shout, saying, *He's had enough, please leave him alone.* I grabbed his long hair at the back of his head and asked him if he'd had enough. He was crying, saying, *Yes, you've broke my nose.* I bounced his face off the ground a couple of times just to make sure he'd had enough, then let him up.

He then started saying to his friends how he could have beat me up if I did not have a skinhead. 'You want another go?' I asked, and to my surprise, he said yes. I gave him a quick one-two on the nose, which finished the fight off, but he still said, while he was walking away, 'I would have beaten you if you had longer hair,' as I put my clothes back on. I was quite happy with myself for the rest of the year.

Not a great deal happened after that, except in the final week. Harry, Sid, and I were just having a laugh going from maths class to woodwork, and this lad bumped into me, turned around and said, 'Watch what you're doing.' I said it was you who bumped me. He's staring at me, saying, *Do what? You want to have a go, like*? I said yes and turned to give Harry my coat.

Harry said, 'Are you serious, he's a fourth year!'

I said yes, smiled, and got stuck into him, but only a minute into this fight and Harry shouted 'Teacher!' so we all split up and walked off. That was good, I said to Harry and Sid, who replied with, 'You're a fucking nutter,' as we all went into woodwork class.

What if?

This was our last lesson, and Harry and I went the same way to the bus stop. As we were walking up the street Albert Toad, hardest lad in the school, came over to us and said to Harry, 'What the fuck you doing picking on one of my mates?'

Harry replied, 'What, mate?' but Albert just headbutted him and said, 'Do it again and it will be a lot worse the next time,' and walked off.

I had to laugh at Harry's face. I said, 'I beat his mates up and you get the clout!' Great fun.

It wasn't until I was 13 though that I stopped just being a scrapper and got into boxing training proper. One time on the way home from school, I was fighting this lad outside Ponteland Garage, laying into one another, when this car pulls up and out gets this massive, fat baldy man. He says to us both to stop brawling on the streets and get ourselves down to West End boys' boxing club. This was Phil Fowler, an ex-Welsh boxing champion and gentleman, and as I showed I was willing to put the hours in at the club, he liked me and wanted me to progress fast. He had me sparring with very good amateur boxing champions and ex-pros, I was good, and of the 11 bouts I had with the club, I won all 11.

One time I remember being in the gym and this lad walked in, his name was John Davinson, he asked me if I would have a couple of rounds sparring, I said yes, we started, and he hit me so hard with a right hook, it wobbled me a little. He asked, 'Are you OK?', I said, 'Yes, no bother,' thinking *Fucking prick*, then I waited for the right time for me to give him my best left hook – that knocked him to the ropes. It done the trick, he said he had had enough. We then decided to go to the community hall, all part of the same building, where all the other kids were dancing and walking around in a big circle. John and I became good friends from this night on. Later, he became the WBO bantamweight champion. I carried on at the West End doing my best, my warm-up was now done on the dance floor to Elvis Presley songs, the coach shouting from the balcony, *Keep in your stance, left foot forward*, this was so funny,

I met my first girlfriend Linda at the club, her friend asked me to dance with them to *Three*

Steps to Heaven. I did, and Linda must have been impressed, and I walked Linda home a few times. Always keeping myself fit, I ran from home to the club and back after training, walking Linda home, and then running a mile or so longer back to my home. This went on 'til I was 16 and a half years old, and then I took a different path.

Almost 16 years old, practising my Bruce Lee moves on Tynemouth beach.

What became of the first crop of F.I.T. Club boxers? Left to right, Peter, doctor; Michael, detective; Mark, SAS; and Kevin, PE teacher (photo taken at High Bridge, 2004).

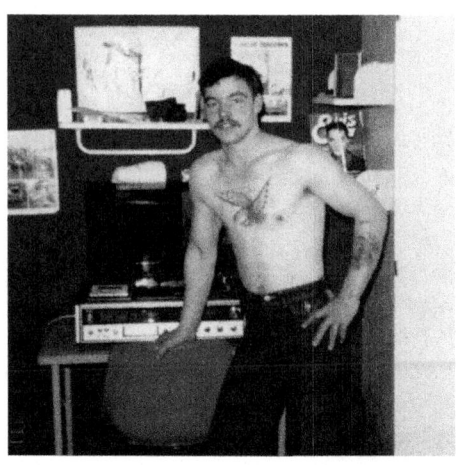

Seventeen-year-old me settling into the Royal Artillery's Plymouth barracks – the tiger's head tattoo is for 'The Sting of the Ring'.

Selection camp at Wiltshire, 1977, for what would be 29 Commando.

Basic training with the RA at
Woolwich training depot, 1976.

Bantamweight win against the Netherlands 1978

Featherweight win for the RA against Germany, 1979, against the German civilian champion.

Lightweight win for the RA against the French civilian champion, France, 1980.

My 26th bout of 62 – a bantamweight fight for the regiment in 1978 – was my second and last loss.

An enjoyable night out as runner-up where I met Gerry of Gerry and the Pacemakers – not, as he pointed out, that Freddie of Freddie and the Dreamers!

Since 2005, I've been keeping civilians fit with military techniques at King Edward's Bay with the infamous Beach Beaster.

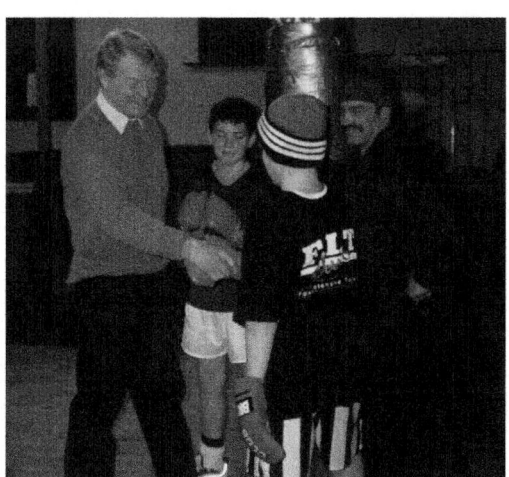

Mr Paddy Ashdown MP, himself formerly of the SBS, came to the Cooperage in 1986 to meet the youngsters at F.I.T. Club.

Pamela, Angela, Maureen, and Denise

Family together brother Bobby, me, David

Church where we got the lead, Cooperage, start, and finish of my employment days

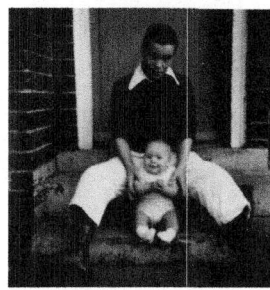 

growing up from Benwell to Blakelaw

Start of business in High Bridge 1999

Team two 10-mile run after assault course

Mam is enjoying a day out at the beach

Dad enjoying his gardening

10-mile Cross Country run for the Regiment RA

Boxing bid to beat childhood obesity

GLOVES ARE ON Boxing is to be introduced to North schools to beat childhood obesity and the gang culture.

Angela, my wife, on the pads for the children's weight loss programme

My newborns, Tyrina (April 1984) and Kevin (November 1985).

CHAPTER 4

BECOMING A MAN

I left school at 16 years with not as much as a last year's report. Signed on at the unemployment office for a couple of months, helped my Mam out doing a bit of cleaning, a little bit of stocking the bars up working at the Cooperage public house on Newcastle's quayside. I also got a job as the tea boy on the building site with my Dad. I was then promoted, having a tea boy under my care as I give him his tasks, and I moved to driving the dumper truck, taking bricks from one end of the site to the other. I was working seven days a week and making £27 for it, giving my Mam £15 board money.

It was when I was 16 I decided to walk into town to the army recruitment office and book a test to

What if?

enlist. I had to have my Mam sign a document to say she authorised me signing up. After about a week, I got a letter asking me to attend an entrance exam, and on that morning, I got the bus into town and sat the exam with 10 other people. We were told to go for lunch and come back for 2 pm to find out the results – I was there for 1.50 pm, praying I had done enough to pass. The recruitment officer called me into his office and congratulated me on my pass, telling me I was one of four out of the 10 who'd made it, and that a member of his staff would go through the next process. I was led to another office where this mountain of a man stood in front of me with my test papers in his hand.

'Well done,' he said. 'Sit down and let's see what job you're looking for in the military.' He asked what kind of soldier I would like to be, and if I had any knowledge of the work the army does, as there were so many options. I told him my Dad and brother David had both served in the army, and I would like to be a PTI in the parachute regiment. He then asked, 'Why the paras?' as there were lots of regiments and all had gymnasiums. I said I like the look, I see the Paras on the news doing stuff all the time. He then said, 'Well, your test results give you a pass to get in the parachute regiment, but there are only three regiments, and everyone is fit and wants to be PTIs. Your results are just over the line for this regiment, and when you go to Canterbury test centre for the two-day test, you will possibly fail and then not be given a chance.' Ah. He said I was better off joining the Royal Artillery and transfer to the 29 Commando regiment or 7 Para regiment RA, adding that if that was OK, we could set up the medical for the next day. I agreed and passed the medical. Two weeks later, I was called in to take the oath, given my Bible and £2.42 travel money – we were told we had to have this amount on us at all times – and was told to wait for my call-up papers. Fantastic! I was in. I got home and told my Mam and Dad, they were so pleased.

Something I need add, though. A couple of years before, when I used to go around and stay at Bobby and Sally's in Kenton, her younger brother Philip was also staying there as he had since their mam had died, and for a while they'd gone into care. We became friends and when I stayed around theirs we'd go out, to the fair, pick up girls, hang out, odds what lads do. One night though staying over, he says he knows a Fine Fare shop nearby with a stash of cigarettes that would be dead easy to nick. So about 3 am we got up, snuck out down the drainpipe and silently jogged through the streets to this shop, opposite which was a patch of common where we lay and spied it all out. After a few minutes, he says he's going for it, I can keep watch for the police, and if I see anyone, whistle, and over he tiptoes, me thinking he's going around the back or something to jemmy a dodgy padlock or whatnot.

Instead, he puts a brick through the front window – great plate glass thing comes down with an almighty *SMASH*, sets off the alarm, and he's inside. I saw a police car coming, but because of the alarm he doesn't hear me whistle, doesn't hear me shout, they're in there and drag him out. I then had to get back to the house and into bed, before the police turn up and tell Bobby and Sally what Philip had done – which they did, but also that only Philip was involved, nothing about me, he'd not told them, which if he had, or I was caught anyway, I'd never have gotten into the army. He was never the sort to grass anyway, but at the time much worse for me I thought was if Bobby had found out. He had such pride and hopes in my development, and it would have hurt him a lot – and then he'd hurt me with a beating.

February 12th, I was on the train to Canterbury for my two days of selection training, got through, put into the combat category, and sent to Woolwich Royal Artillery training barracks. While all the other troop contingents had one drill sergeant, ours, Colenso Troop, had two bombardiers. I fitted in very well with all the lads and the instructors, I was the smallest and the fittest in the troop. Only two of us had boxed before, and we were given the position of troop leaders, assigned with getting the jobs done by assigning the best person for that job. This position had its benefits by means of time management, to get things done faster, so the troop could work better and harder with our personal kit. Three months of training and it was nothing short of brilliant.

I had two boxing bouts for the troop, winning both, the first being a preliminary bout to the final, and was a total mismatch. He must have been about two stone heavier, a foot taller, but, as

What if?

I was told, I was put up because I had experience. I knocked him down twice in the first round, and three times in the second, and still it went to the judges – what a fix! – although I got the decision. We learn you have to deal with what's in front of you, no matter what, and you will find out the harder you work and the more you want it, you will win.

That hard work and determination will pay dividends came true as I made it to the end of training, Mam and Dad, and two sisters coming to the passing out parade. I was in the front rank on display to everyone, so proud of achieving this goal, not having an education, and still having passed the exam stage was great. After the inspection on the parade square, we quickly got to the gymnasium, into our sportswear, and lined up to do our gymnastic display in front of our audience. I was in the gymnastics squad for the end of passing out parade because I could do a handstand, handspring using the vaulting platform, and somersault over the pommel horse from my diving and trampolining at school. My Dad was so proud, talking to everyone of how fit and disciplined a lad I was. We were all allowed to go home for two weeks' leave before joining our regiments. Unfortunately, I was the only one from the troop to get the Commando posting, to 29 Commando based in Plymouth, again a new beginning for me. While on leave, I had a few more boxing bouts, again winning all. I was selected to box for the Battery, the regiment, and later the army, at various weights against opponents both military and civvy, and had a great time. I think I travelled more with the boxing squads than in uniform, going to Germany three times, Spain, France, and the Netherlands.

As a Commando, there is a lot to cover, from the beat up selection week, training, getting your wings as a paratrooper, then further training.

For arctic warfare, I had an experience in Bavaria, Germany, with this training mission to rescue a general held captive in the middle of a forest. We parachuted 15 miles out of the area, regrouped into two sets of five commandos – always on the lookout for possible ambush – it took six days to reach our objective, this being because the snow was up to two feet deep and very soft, every step had to be taken without the snow crunching,

What if?

as well as the possibility of trip wires that could have been laid anywhere en route. We took turns in sleeping, digging a hole in the snow like an igloo, putting up a bivi and stripping naked, and slipping into your sleeping bag, your combats in the sleeping bag with you to stay dry and warm, getting your stove out and cooking your meal, making sure you did not have the light from the stove reflecting outwards to give your position away. Next task was to have your helmet filled with melted snow for a wash and a shave, making sure all main areas of the body were cleaned, changing your socks and undies. When everyone was ready, we travelled onwards, the closer we got to our objective, the less sleep and rest we had. For the last three days as we got closer to the position we were moving so slowly, using only hand signals.

Within 200 yards of the cabin where the general was being held, eight guards were on the outside, and the intelligence we had was the general was being held in a room at the back of this cabin with a further two guards. One of our two groups took a further five hours to move around the area so we had totally surrounded the cabin, three lads on both teams moved in and took out six outer guards with the technique of cutting the tendon at the back of the knee and the person automatically falling backwards, allowing for strangulation, preventing any screaming and no chance of a weapon being fired. The two closest to the cabin door were drawn away with the noise of one of the other guards falling, a little sloppy work, but it worked as these two were also taken down without a shot being fired. Everyone was now grouped, ready for the big rush, as we waited for about an hour for one of the guards inside to open the door to give instructions to one of his colleagues. We burst in and rescued the general who was having a nice hot cup of tea. End of mission, and it was well documented as a very successful one.

I then had the privilege of taking a short, three-day training course in skiing in central Norway to learn how to cope in arctic warfare on skis. I put on the skis, having never put a pair of skis on before this training, and was instructed to stand at the top of this hill. I was waiting for instruction to move, and then a big boot kicked me up the arse, and I shot off like a bullet, it was so funny as I just stayed in the squat position all the way

What if?

down about a half mile. Then I was called to basecamp to get kicked off the course, being told I was fucking useless, and I was flown out back to camp to get on a plane to Belize for jungle warfare, and I done better at that.

It was a fantastic experience, training with all these professionals. For jungle warfare, we had to acclimatise to the tropical climate, deal with storms where it rained heavily for two, three days, but as always, it was a great education. Then, a short stop in Brunei, having fun with the Gurkha regiment, what an incredible, disciplined group of soldiers. Working in the jungle, we could only move about 100 meters in about 20 minutes through the thick growth in temperatures of 35 degrees-plus. Living in these conditions tests you in every sense possible.

Looking back now over my life, all these start-stops of new beginnings, having to build up the courage and dealing with disappointment along the way, have given me the attitude to have a go at anything, and if it works, carry on; if it fails, carry on. Don't be beat by setbacks, people will always make their own judgment of you, good or bad, and does it matter? No, it does not, as long as you're true to yourself.

I always help people and ask for no reward, but some, not all people in your life, will push and push for you to change your values just to get the upper hand. I am now 65 years old and not happy with every decision I have made to help others, just for getting a kick in the teeth for it. But I still help people, just having learnt all the time, I have become a little more selective of who I help.

The army is built on everyone helping others, the attitude is, 'One fails, we all fail.' Never leave a man behind, and always be familiar with what your buddy is doing in his job role, in case he is not able to carry it out on a mission. I had a brilliant time serving with a great bunch of lads. I took my PTI course in 1978 and loved it.

Then though, I had a fight with a fellow soldier (different regiment, he was serving in the Royal Green Jackets). He said a really bad thing about my mother, and I ended up really going to town on this big bastard, went berserk, put him through a shop window.

What if?

I was demoted and put in Colchester prison, known as Colchester Glasshouse, for 186 days, before being returned to 29 Commando full of life, as the prison time I spent was brilliant! Every day, from locker inspection was 40 40-minute guards drill, which I loved, 40 minutes exercise, drill, exercise, through to bedtime, lights out at 10 pm. Sunday was either washing and ironing day for one of the six lads in our dormitory, everyone else was at church. Breakfast: half a fried egg, one rasher of bacon, one sausage, and a spoonful of beans, and a boiling hot half cup of tea. Lunch: small scoop of potato, pork chop, a spoon of peas, and a very hot cup of tea. Supper was a little more elaborate: two roast potatoes, cabbage, carrots, beef, and gravy. At the end of every meal, there was only one person allowed to stand up. It was a case of spin the salt cellar, and if it landed on you, then you're taking all the plates back to the kitchen while everyone else gets on parade. I fully enjoyed my time at the Glasshouse, it was true discipline.

My further education in the army came with two tours of Northern Ireland. I was posted in Armagh and Tyrone. As an observer, I dug in for two, three months at a time, watching members of a loyalist group, mostly from Northern Ireland, who carried out shooting and bombing attacks against Catholics and nationalists during the Troubles, but I can't say much except it was tough.

I was returned to the unit to box for the regimental championships. This was going to be a tough show, as my surveillance duty meant I had not done any training for two months. I got back to camp early morning around 4 am, then up for 8 am, out for a run, got weighed in for 10 am, to find I was 10 grams over the mark of 56 kg. The opposition team would not accept the bout for then, as they knew the more fitness training I needed to do to lose the weight, the more tired I'd be in the ring and the better their man's chances, if not having to forfeit the fight altogether.

I had to lose the weight within an hour, this was the regulation, so into my combats and boots, and off we went for a run for 45 minutes, before a check weigh-in – I was 2 grams over! The coach said, 'You're going to have a crap or something as we don't have time.' I went to the toilet and forced a poo out the size of a pea – but it done the trick, I made the weight, and then we went for a well-earned breakfast, steak and eggs, and a good sleep.

I had my preliminary bout at 2 pm, and then the final at 8 pm. I won the first bout quite easy against a Welsh lad, he had held a Welsh title and a regimental title, score was outstanding, given the circumstances, 20-15, 20-12, 20-16 in my favour, and the second bout was against another Welsh lad, who held a couple of championship titles. It was pretty even in the first round, with a good steady flow of punches both ways, and it was also pretty even in the second, even though I was now starting to feel the bite of the lack of training. Third round, he pipped it by one point, score was 20-20, 20-20, 20-19 in his favour. I got the best runner-up trophy, but I was gutted after the presentation.

I went in the toilets and cried for about 10 minutes, disappointed with this performance. The lads from the troop came in and got me out for a celebration of the night, but the lesson I learned was always keep fit, as had I have come in on weight I would have taken the two bouts. We went to Tiffany's nightclub, where Gerry and the Pacemakers were having a gig, unknown to me, but being on the drink, I was looking for bother, as I was still upset about the performance,

I started asking for Gerry, and he come flying over the tables and stood right in front of me, asking what did I want. Looking confused I said, 'You're not fucking Gerry, where's your moustache and glasses?'

He said, 'You're meaning Freddie and the Dreamers.' Oh, hmmm, I said, agreeing with him, so we sat down and had a pint together. He said, 'Next show you have, give me a call, and I will come and present the trophies,' and then that was the end of the night.

Over the years, my boxing record in and outside of the army would be 62 bouts, including my juniors' bouts, of which I won 60, with 24 stoppages, 19 by way of knockout. I was asked if I would like to turn professional, but declined as this was my hobby, not a living. Also when in the army I was also very much a team player in our regimental rugby team as hooker, and our tug-of-war team. All this, as well as being a soldier – what a brilliant place to be!

But the good things came with the job we were trained to do. In early 1982, Argentina invaded the Falkland Islands. Our battery was deployed on operation in support of 3 Commando Brigade and we were to go for Knob Island, enclaved in the southwest corner of West Falkland. Once it had been checked out by the SBS, we were placed there as observers, with lads from 148 Commando also manning our operational position (OP). From here, we plotted a list of targets on the main island, radioing them back to *HMS Plymouth*, which took up position on its gun line and proceeded to shell Argentine fuel stores and ammo dumps. We were also included in the Pebble Island Raid with D Squadron, 22 SAS, and the assault with 2 Para on Goose Green.*

This was a little naughty episode in my military career, by naughty I mean horrible, as my buddy Scouse was shot in the eye by a ricocheted bullet. It looked like half his face was blown off, and as I was next to him, I was covered with blood. I quickly grabbed a bandage and got his cap, comforter, and beret to help with the dressing, applying the pressure needed to slow down the bleeding. He kept fainting, going in and out of consciousness. I radioed for assistance from the medical team, who were there in minutes and stretchered him away, and then we moved forward with the on the Pebble Island raid. We were picked up by *HMS Plymouth,* and we all got time to get some well-deserved rest. I called Scouse before I left for England. He had lost his eye and needed bone reconstruction on his eye socket, but said he was doing great and was in good humour. I was awarded a medal for my actions, but always thought, 'Why?' – it's my job, this is what we do for each other.

My Dad died during my service. This was so hard to accept, as he was so tough and a fighter to the core, but lost his battle to cancer that I hadn't even been aware he had cancer. I put in a request to buy myself out, to help look after my Mam and get her settled, and then went to re-enlist three month later. But after the Falklands War, the government was cutting back on the service personnel, so I was stuck on leaving the army, never to return to the job I loved.

CHAPTER 5

THE BUSINESS

I tried for employment with the police, but I was too short at 5' 4". I tried for a position as a PTI in the prison service, but no vacancies. I was asked if I wanted to be a PE teacher, but with having to sit exams to qualify, this was not for me.

I was lost, no one to turn to, put in a place that had no walls, no protection, no buddies. Again, I had to start from the beginning. Seven years of training being part of a fantastic organisation, it was like having a big mother with you every step of the way. And then being a civilian, everyone for themselves, fighting each other, pulling each other down at the first chance, not willing to help others worse off. No respect for anything.

After a couple of months back home, I helped my Mam again at the Cooperage, cleaning to help with board money. I bought a little Mini car to help me get around to find a job, then sold it to buy a Hillman Imp, and this car was where I learnt to do mechanics, taking the engine out, changing broken parts, all from a book, as the Mini was costing too much to run. I then sold the Hillman and bought an Avenger, sold that to get an ex-post office van to use as a removal van, made a few quid doing this, then moved into selling eggs, going from door to door, 40 pence a half-dozen, 60 pence a dozen and £1.00 a tray of 24 eggs.

I thought this was doing great, from two big boxes a week to almost 10 boxes a week, having all the old ladies, ready at the door with their little egg boxes and a lovely smile, showing their appreciation by getting their family members to put orders in, business building every week, then I took a week away with my girlfriend Dawn – my childhood sweetheart who I'd gotten back with – and asked my brother David to look after the deliveries for me, as he was also off work.

What if?

To come back from my week away to find he had not done the deliveries after his first day, him saying, 'You can't make money from this,' it took the wind out of me. I was devastated, sick to think all those little old ladies and their families that were depending on this service to be let down without notice. I did not have the heart to pick it back up, so I put this down as a letdown and not to trust anyone with anything of mine.

I then changed the van for a flat-back pickup that I used to collect scrap, old washing machines, dryers, and so forth. I had two young lads working with me, and for them I opened bank accounts and put their wages into the bank each week. They were over the Moon, this little business was doing very well, made a couple of thousand pounds a month, but the pickup was starting to cost a lot in repairs, so I had to get rid of this and bought a car – which I then sold to get married to Dawn in 1984.

With Dawn, we had two lovely kids, and both have done very well at school. My daughter is a veterinarian surgical nurse, and my son is an architect, and I'm very proud of them both for enjoying school and becoming professionals.

Meanwhile, I was offered a job by my wife's uncle as a labourer at a roof light company. I took the job and within a couple of month I was put on helping the fabricators put their work together, as I was always asking questions and willing to learn, and I was then put on to fabricate on my own, tack welding the pieces together. I took these two jobs on, before being put on night shift as a supervisor to run the factory with 20 lads. 'Why stop there?' I thought, and pushed to keep learning and working hard. After picking these jobs up with ease, I was then asked to be the first to operate in the company's new factory as a pipe bender and a track welder.

I was promoted to supervisor with a squad of 48 workers building £1 million jobs, however, the owner was a rally car owner/driver who had three of these very expensive Audi Quattro cars, and a Golden Socket award-winning mechanic looking after them. The owner smashing them up every week took its toll, meanwhile the business went into administration two years after I started, and we all got paid off.

As I went back on the dole, now married with a daughter, the unemployment office asked if I

What if?

would like to take an exam to get on a City and Guilds fabrication and welding course. After talking with Dawn, we agreed if I could pass the exam, then I would take on the course, a six-month course down in Wakefield, Leeds. I was very nervous about the exam, it was all maths related, but I done enough to get through to take the course, moving south and coming home every weekend. Hard as it was traveling by coach back and forth, I sat seven City and Guilds exams, along with a coded welding certificate, and passed them all, thinking, 'Well, we are in the money now,' as I applied for the oil rigs, only to be informed that I did not have the experience. Again, I was on the dole.

CHAPTER 6

THE START OF THE F.I.T. CLUB

I went back to the Cooperage for the third time in my life, doing some cleaning in the public bar, but took a different tack. I asked the director, Richard, whose brother Michael was the managing director of the whole place, if we could have a job and finish. He asked what I meant, and I said, rather than my Mam and I staying for five to six hours making the job last so we could make our wages up, we would come in early doors and be finished on the ground floor before him and Michael come in. He agreed if the work did not suffer. I then made it with my Mam that I would be in at 6 am in the mornings and have everything done, and she could come in at 8 am to pick up the small piles of muck, and end up doing about 45 minutes' work and getting six hours' pay. It worked great, I was so happy for her.

Then I was asked if I would try the grill chef role, doing burgers and chips for the nightclub. I took these jobs on cleaning through the day 6 am till 9 am, with my Mam coming in for a little under an hour just to show them she was there, and then me cooking from 8 pm 'til 2 am. I thought, why not do the cleaning while there was nothing happening in the kitchen. If an order came in, I could quickly cook and deliver to the nightclub.

I asked Richard if, once the public bar was closed at 10.30 pm, could I start cleaning, he said OK, and then as the cleaning was being done, I asked if my Mam could come in during the night to help me and in the kitchen – again, no problem. My Mam was now making four times the money for the same time she was working on the cleaning.

Richard liked the way I operated and asked me if I would like to become a barman. Yes was the answer. After a good few months learning the bar skills, I asked about the cellar operation, changing barrels, stock taking, which I was shown, all the while working on the bar and covering the cooking and cleaning at the nightclub. Richard was a very lazy person, always leaving the cellar 'til the next morning, never cashing up, just throwing all the money into bags into the safe, leaving Michael the MD the job of counting it next day. This was not the way I work, as leaving your job to others is not good business.

So I started asking this director if he wanted to go home early, as I can finish off. He took the bait, and this happened for a few months, and I was promoted to shift manager. I then took control of the hours available to cover as much as possible, with the cleaning, cooking, and managerial duties all done in a shift – working the bar, keeping on top of the cellar, having Mam cook for the nightclub, cleaning and cashing up neatly, all the bills into the safe, after the bar closed, finishing the cellar, and I was away home by 4 am. This also meant that the next morning, the MD only had to pick the money out of the safe, bank it, then switch on the cellar pumps, and his job was done, saving him hours in his day.

What if?

I was made manager. This was an opportunity to make big changes to the bar staff and mainly the door staff, as both were in cahoots with each other in fiddles. Things like I saw the doorman would have women show them their knickers or stocking tops for free entry, or bar staff charging on the drinks, and not ringing in the full number of drinks, pocketing the difference. At a meeting with the bar personnel, I dismissed the thieving culprits with no arguments. The senior bar staff I finished with and replaced straight away, giving junior staff members a little more responsibility. Worked perfectly, and a lot more money was there to count.

I then called the head doorman into the middle bar and told him I was not happy with his conduct, and he should leave his post straight away. This was 8 pm on a Friday night, not realising that once I said to him he was finished, he would then become the hard man and decided to make a noise. I asked him if he wanted to take it further, 'We could do it right here, right now, no witnesses.' He declined the offer and asked if he could say goodbye to the remainder of the door staff – nine of them – I said fine, but the outcome was not a good one as they all walked out with him.

Oh, shit. The nightclub was starting at 10 pm. So I decided to do the front door myself and called my two brothers in to cover the cashpoint and the back door. Thank God there was no bother whatsoever, not even a spilt drink. Now, I employed my own bar staff and door staff, me taking charge of the door, as I believe leading from the front is the way forward. We cut the amount of drug dealers and takers within the Cooperage and made it a better, happier place to work.

Still we had three, maybe four fights a night, but everyone I give the option, either they could walk out and return the next day, with an apology, and be in the following week – or, be put out and barred for three month, unless they turned up to train with me in the gym I set up in 1986 on the Cooperage nightclub dance floor, what I termed as 'Fast Intensive Training – Clive's Little Ultimate Burner', or F.I.T. Club. Some took up the offer to come in for training to get back in, but little did they know how hard the training was.

What if?

With opening time in the nightclub not 'til 10 pm, I set the gym up at 5 pm to start training at 5.30 pm with the ladies class, taking them out for a run, doing the stairs and banks around the Quayside, then back to the Cooperage gym for the bag and floor workout, finishing for 6.15 pm and then the lads 6.30-7.30 pm before the parties that were booked in the nightclub. Monday was a general session, a little of everything, but Tuesday was just arms – a good 20-minute run hitting the stairs and hills, doing press ups up the wooden stairs opposite the Copthorne Hotel (all 92 of them) with a platform in the middle allowing for wheelbarrow walks to the next set and changing with your partner, then back to the gym to finish with a press up circuit. Wednesday was just midsection, after a good run we found a hill and lay down, head downhill, and your partner holding your feet for sit-ups, then back to the gym for a midsection workout. Thursday was all legs: a one-hour run hitting all the hills and stairs on the Quayside, then a hill workout with a fireman's carry up and down the hill, back to the gym for squats with your partner on your back. Fridays were a normal workout, and Sundays a gentle two-hour squad training. About 15, 20 people did the classes, kids too, and we got our own branded kit made for the regulars.

While running the nightclub, I was still competing in boxing, so I had to stay on top of my game – no smoking, no drinking, just work, and fitness was the medicine. But out of all the fights and people being put out, there was one incident that took the biscuit.

I'd been manager for about four years when one Saturday night, there was a nice, quiet Scottish lad, or so he appeared, he came to the door to get into the nightclub. He was on his own, and the doorman let him in for a couple of drinks. Later that night, around 2.15 am, while everyone was leaving, this lad decided to have an argument with two blokes, who also had a good drink. They were ushered to the middle floor below the nightclub on their way to being ejected, when the Scottish lad decided to pull out a 9" knife from the back of his belt. I was halfway down the stairs when I saw the knife and shouted to everyone *Move out of the way!* as he went for the two other lads. I saw an opportunity without endangering me or my staff, and I signalled to the two door staff closest

What if?

to him, then I kicked the hand with the knife in it, they grabbed him and took the knife off him.

One of the doormen carried the lad to the top of the stairs, where he tried to break free and fell headfirst down the stairs. He lay at the bottom of the stairs motionless, blood coming out of his left ear. I told the bar staff to call an ambulance and tried to give comfort to the lad, trying not to move him as he came down the stairs at some speed. The ambulance arrived, and I asked what hospital he would be going to so I could check to see if he was OK. The two doormen involved in the disarming of the lad stayed back and talked about the way things happened, but were in total shock, and as we talked the story became different every time we went over it. I said we need to have it clear, and all have the same view of what happened. About 90 minutes later, the police arrived to take statements, as this was now cause for concern. In fact, the lad died in hospital about three hours later.

The doorman in question was charged with manslaughter, It was also mentioned, the bar staff had asked me if the lad could buy a 1.5-litre bottle of vodka, as this would be cheaper than by the normal measure. As a business decision, I said yes to the bottle being sold for £20 to the Scottish lad, with strict instructions – that it be served in normal measures each time, no more, and to observe the customer's behaviour. Neither of these instructions had been obeyed. I was in charge and tried to protect my staff for giving bigger measures than they should have, but the doormen's stories varied, as they both melted under pressure.

I took the responsibility, and I was charged with perverting the course of justice. Took a year and a half for the trial to get to the Crown Court, and I was suspended during all this time. The doorman got off with the manslaughter charge, as the lad was known to the Scottish police for causing similar offences up there. And because he did not die at the bottom of the stairs, but he died in hospital after leaving the Cooperage, the doorman was found not guilty, as was I. Then I was allowed to return to work. A new staircase was ordered by the court to be erected in the Cooperage as the original was seen to be too steep.

What if?

It was only a few months before the director was paid off and went to set up a bar in York, and I was made general manager of the Cooperage – the pub, restaurant, and nightclub. Six months passed, and the new staircase was ready to put in place, meaning the nightclub and restaurant were closed for about eight weeks, so the MD and his wife went on holiday, leaving me in charge of the bar, the MD being on the end of the phone to deal with the builders. As they were on holiday, I was approached by Newcastle Breweries to work for them, with fantastic terms and conditions and pay, and after the MD got back from his three-week break, I gave my notice, recommending one of my duty managers to take over.

At a brewery training pub in Wallsend, I then spent two weeks learning more about running a bar, but while I was doing great with that, my wife called to tell me my wages from the Cooperage had not been paid into the bank. This caused quite a few financial problems, with credit cards, mortgage, school fees, etc, and I phoned the MD and asked why had my wages not gone into the bank. He said it was his wife's decision to post a cheque out, covering the days worked, as I had not completed a full month. I was furious, and drove straight to the Cooperage. The MD was there and said we would have to go along to the office to see his wife, who would explain. I got in the office to see her sitting behind her desk, and with a big, stupid smile on her face, she asked, 'What seems to be the problem?'

'Why did you not just let the payment go into the bank as normal, and if I had been overpaid, call me to pay back the difference?'

'You left us,' she said, 'and you have been paid. It's not my fault you have financial problems to deal with. You have a cheque, which will clear in three days.'

I could not hold back the rage, threw the cheque in her face as the MD stood there saying, 'Clive please calm down, we can sort this out, please Clive,' like he's almost crying, as I picked up one side of her desk and tipped it over, shouting, *I will throw you through the fucking window, you fucking slut*! She ran into the corner of the office shouting to the MD, *Stop him, call the police! Call the police*! I realised it was not going to end well for her or me … so I walked out of the office.

What if?

Down the stairs, the MD came in tow, said he wanted to give the wages I was due, and also give me a £1,000 for all the work and support. I told him, 'Get my money in the bank today,' and to stick the £1,000 up his wife's arse. I headed back to Wallsend, where I was met by the area manager, given a public house in Fenham, the Balloon, with a three-bedroom flat upstairs to it.

I ran the Balloon with great intentions of having my own pub one day, for my wife and kids, Tyrina (by then 6) and Kevin (5). But the pub was in a troubled place, between Slatyford, Blakelaw, and Cowgate, all deprived areas, with the bar always breaking out in fights, and me having to deal with it all. Needing to keep myself fit, I built a gym in the cellar because of all the bother I was having. Some of the customers were trying to take liberties, causing trouble, not listening to what I was telling them, and I would take them down in the cellar, give them a good beating, and bar them for a week, but all this went on for nine month.

Then the MD from the Cooperage came to see me and ask if I would consider returning to my old job, as the place had taken a slide in sales once

I left – the bar was doing OK, but the restaurant and nightclub were on the verge of closing down. I said yes – with three conditions: 1) Same wages I left on; 2) Give me more freedom to run the business; and 3) Keep his wife well out of my fucking way. He agreed.

It took me a year to get the Cooperage back to full strength, doing brilliant deals with breweries, selling low-cost bottled beers at nightclub prices, taking the Cooperage from £18k a week total to £25k a week and £15k at the weekend. The bar was full almost every night, the restaurant full day and night, we had theme nights on through the week, Valentines, Mothers' Day, Fathers' Day, Burns Night, Spanish Armada night, a French theme event with Beaujolais Nouveau. Easy to make money when you're willing to put the graft in. On the back of this, I always had my gym running, 90 minutes before the nightclub opened, and on Sunday afternoon, keeping myself fit for all the fights that took place in the club.

As the Cooperage was doing so well, the MD and his wife decided to take early retirement and sell to Bass Breweries. The MD secured my job and position, but it was a total change going from a free-trade public house to being told by letter what you had to order and sell. I had won so many awards for cellar management, biggest sales on beers in the country, all that, but the two years I worked for Bass, I had no control whatsoever and didn't like it. But while running the Cooperage for Bass, I took a six-month business management course through Business Link, and at Gateshead College, did a two-year part-time course to update my PTI certificate, as well as running fitness classes before and after the parties and the nightclub.

Most of the lads and lasses who trained with me were from local areas, Benwell, Gateshead, so on, and I opened a slot at a local community centre to keep them fit, with about 20 regulars paying £1 per class, although about half left when I was charged extra for room hire and raised the fee to £1.50 (well, the Cooperage gym was only 20 pence a session – and that included a drink of orange).

But not all was going so well. My marriage to Dawn had been troubled for a while, and we divorced in 1996. And working for Bass was a nightmare. I had to make a decision – move on, set up my own company. And so gave birth to my own proper gym, getting F.I.T. Club into its own premises on High Bridge, Newcastle, with a 15-year lease.

Moving to High Bridge was extremely expensive, but I negotiated a 12-month rent-free period, and it was going to be worth the stress. The premises were on the first floor, just an open space with lots of work to do, with my kids, Kevin and Tyrina doing a footfall count and asking people what they would like from a gym in town.

Some wanted fitness, weights, boxing, ladies-only classes, and men-only classes. I partitioned the space off with a reception, small office, toilets, a small weightlifting gym, and a big open boxing gym, with six punchbags and an 11x11 foot boxing ring.

Setting up the gym took almost six months, during which time I was sleeping at the premises so I could work overnight. My bank business consultant told me to sign on the dole for unemployment benefit at £37.00 week, the catch being I had to be seen to be looking for employment – stupid as it all was, I was told that setting up my own business to employ myself was not thought of as looking for work.

As I could not understand this logic, I carried on signing on, taking in my self-made letters of proposed interviews and my self-made rejection letters, and the people behind the desk of the dole accepted them as proof of looking for work. This carried on until my bank account was opened and the gym was set to open its doors, which we did on 1st June, 1999. One of the council officers came with a reporter from *The Chronicle* newspaper to market the opening, but unfortunately, they were the only people that turned up! Not one person that I had trained for the 12 years that I was at the Cooperage to celebrate the opening. I took this as, 'You are on your own, mate! Dig in, and get on with it.'

The gym was very slow to start, then it began picking up with the ladies' classes, mainly office workers, then the lads' classes got really busy. I was charging £3 per class. Then one old gentleman came in for a session, once he had finished his class, said, 'I really enjoyed that, son. Do you know that you would have to pay a fortune to get a workout like that? Please don't underprice your talent, as for me, if this lot are willing to pay £3, they will be willing to pay £5 per class.' OK, I thought, then he said: 'Don't be a fool and try to fit everyone's pocket, because when they're ready to leave you, they will, without a thought about your finances.' How true this was. Just thinking of all the times I helped people at the Cooperage, and at this place was using credit cards to pay my way through, still trying to look after people with discounts. And not one had turned up to support me on the big day.

As he said, clients came and went, it was a fast turnover, and after 12 months with rent of £700 a month now looming atop the other overheads, I put the price up. But it was taking off. I then started to put runs on around the area, about 30 minutes before the session started, then set up competitive runs for the clients: a 10-mile jelly tea run, 14-mile beach run, 20-mile Cheviot run, half-marathons, and so on, which again kept the customers happy and got a regular turnout, and I started organising charity events like abseiling from the Tyne Bridge, assault courses, and so on.

What if?

I took a boxing coaching course and set up an amateur boxing club with the Amateur Boxing Association in 2004, and started to put my lads into competition, which I did for several years. This had its rewards as I was getting more people coming through the door, buying gloves, headgear, gumshields, as well as water. I was open from 10 am till 10 pm Monday to Friday, Saturday 10 'til 2, as things progressed I was asked if I would take a half-dozen Russian students who wanted private morning classes. Then I took on a Muslim group of about 10 people, mornings, and then a group of Turkish lads, mornings, so now, as well as my normal clients, I had these three sets of clients coming in, money coming in, the business was now paying the bills.

Then I thought it would be good that, instead of buying gloves retail and selling them on through the club shop with a discount, to expand the F.I.T. Club clothing range and start importing all my own gloves and bags with my logo on, like we'd had on our boxing tops and all since the Cooperage, and sell it all through the gym and online under the name F.I.T. Club Gear Limited. I travelled to Pakistan, India, China, and Thailand in search of good manufacturers while my girlfriend Angela, who I'd met at the Cooperage in '98, took time off her work at the HMRC to cover the gym in my absence. I was now on the boxing circuit, taking my lads to shows to compete, and I could do a little selling at the same time, and quite a few clubs were buying regular through their Lottery grants. Then it all turned sour, as a few clubs were saying that anyone who was buying off me was just financing the F.I.T. Club itself, even though the apparel was under F.I.T. Club Gear Limited.

I changed the apparel company logo to FCG Boxing, thinking this would bring back the sales, but the main boxing club coaches had made sure that no one was going to buy from me. Meanwhile, after two years, I became a boxing judge, lining me up with a three-month course three years to become a boxing referee. This gave me a little more influence to sell my gear, mainly to the Newcastle-based clubs. But it then got to a stage that I was out officiating more than I was running my own club, costing £600 a year for the registration, £100 for the official, (me) and £100 for the coaches (me again, paying for *me* to do *my* job). I was on duty judging or refereeing three, sometimes four, times a week and that on top of trying to run my business and getting out to the shows. It was all becoming too trying, my lads were missing their training. And so after 14 years I decided to pull out of the Amateur Boxing Association.

I then set up charity boxing shows that I was in total control of. Boxers would need to register and purchase the competition gear from F.I.T. Club Gear, now just FCG, so the logo fits on the gloves. All the advertising for the F.I.T. Club was free, and all other businesses that sponsored the show paid for their logos to be put up in the venue or on the programs. I then set up my third wholesale company as FCG Apparel Limited, with a new logo and sponsoring the boxing shows, giving it more advertising. How I looked at it was FC Apparel bought the gear from the manufacturer, then FCG would buy the gear wholesale from FC Apparel, and sell it to F.I.T. Club for retail at discounted prices. Everything was within one group of companies owned and run by me.

For the boxing shows, I would select a charity, mostly the Children's Heart Foundation, as my niece has had to have several cardiac surgeries since she was born, sometimes giving boxers or customers an opportunity to suggest charities close to their own hearts, say for a family member or friend with a condition. Since the first bout, we have raised over £200,000 for charities. I try and have two shows a year, not always possible due to injuries, sickness, bail outs, but as well as raising awareness and funds for the charities we support, we give people the chance to partake in actual boxing, something that would not otherwise be possible for them on the licenced amateur boxing circuit because for reasons like age, ability, or confidence.

Out of all the customers that have passed through the gym, only two would cause me to get angry. One guy at a F.I.T. Club Christmas party decided to chat my girlfriend Angela up, and asked her for a date. She took no time in telling me what he said, but it took him around three month to turn back up to the gym. With the gym full with around 30 customers waiting to go for a run, he walked into reception with his mate and went straight into the changing room. I waited until he put his head in the gym and asked if I could

What if?

have a word outside the door at the top of the stairs, and he come out with me, not suspecting anything, as he must have thought he done no wrong. I asked, 'Why did you ask Angela out for a date?' He said he could not remember as he was pissed. I asked again, why did he ask Angela out on a date. Same answer: 'I was pissed,' he claimed. Not a good enough answer for me, so I headbutted him on the nose, and as he put his hands to his face, I spun him around and threw him headfirst down the stairs, him landing on his back. I followed him down to make sure he was not going to get away without a good slap, and as with previous fights, I gave him a few kicks to the ribs, then got a hold of his fat head, bounced it off the floor and dragged him into the street off the premises, then told his pal, *Get the fuck out of my gym and take that daft prick with you.* He had to take him to hospital, but he did not grass, told the police he had been beat up across in Gateshead.

The other customer was one of my boxers, who offended Angela – by then my wife, we married in 2015 – by telling her to *fuck off* when she asked him to stop jumping around in the gym, as he was going to kick or hurt someone. She told me the next day. I asked him if I could have a word in the reception area, he agreed and stood with his hands on his hips, and I asked why he was being rude and disrespectful to Angela. He said, 'She's got the attitude.'

As I moved a little closer, he tried to grab me, so I throat-punched him, and as he was starting to choke, I headbutted him. *I have had enough, I will get my gear and leave*, he said, but as he walked in the gym to get his gear, he start making a noise, saying *Your fucking sessions are shite anyway*. We got to the top of the stairs and he was about four steps down, saying *I was fucking leaving anyway*.

'Do you want to have a go?' I asked. He claimed he couldn't possibly have a go fighting me as I was too old and had grey hair. I was just at the right height to kick him under the chin, so I did, and backwards he fell down the stairs, getting on his feet only to run out the front door. I did not bother to chase him as it was off the premises. Job done.

CHAPTER 7

THE END GAME

After 22 years of having just the one gymnasium, in 2021, I took the opportunity to take on another property suitable for my second gym and called it CGPTI Limited, my personal training gym. Having sold two other properties to fund this project, and have since had a steady flow of clients, but have found it impossible to find the instructors to take my place, as no one is dedicated enough to take on the role – they are only interested in the money, not the clients. So I decided to do it myself, less hassle.

Life's been amazing, while I wonder, for all the incredible twists and turns, what could have gone so differently for want of a second, if not a day later here, or another decision there. As it is, I've got two beautiful little dogs, Winston and Churchill, that need to be considered for their comfort and life, before making the move for my or Angela's retirement. Very well earned it'll be, too.